The Last of the
CHEJU DIVERS

Rob Waring, *Series Editor*

T0354110

HEINLE
CENGAGE Learning

Australia • Brazil • Japan • Korea • Mexico • Singapore • Spain • United Kingdom • United States

Words to Know

This story is set in South Korea. It happens in a place called Cheju [tʃeɪdʒuː] Island.

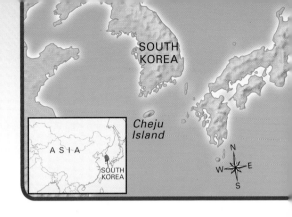

A **Scuba Divers.** Label the picture with the <u>underlined</u> words in the paragraph.

   Divers are people who go underwater for enjoyment or their job. <u>Scuba divers</u> use an <u>oxygen tank</u>. It allows them to breathe underwater. Sometimes divers go into the <u>sea</u> to find <u>seafood</u>. Octopus, abalone, and sea urchin are common seafoods.

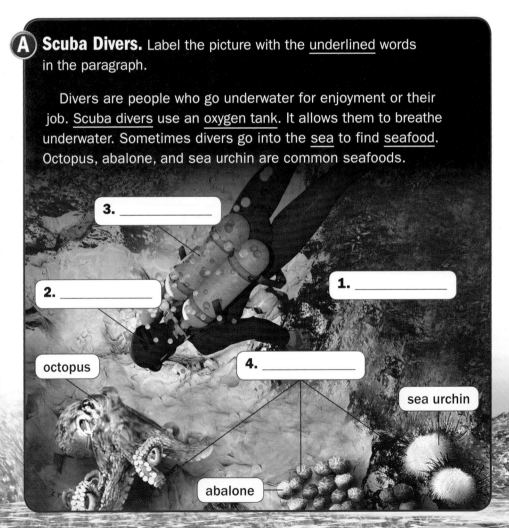

3. _____

2. _____

1. _____

octopus

4. _____

sea urchin

abalone

B Cheju Divers. Read the paragraph. Then match each word with the correct definition.

Cheju is a small island that is known for its legendary women divers. It's also a society that is changing. In the past, women in Cheju often had to become divers, or *Haenyos* [haɪnjoʊs], to get money. It was dangerous, but there was no other way to make a living. Recently, more tourists have been coming to the island. The young women of Cheju now have more job choices. This story is about the differences between these two generations of women. It's about a young tour guide and her 63-year-old aunt, who is one of the last of the Cheju divers.

1. legendary _____	**a.** a visitor who travels for enjoyment
2. make a living _____	**b.** people of a similar age within a society or family
3. tourist _____	**c.** the sister of someone's father or mother
4. choice _____	**d.** possibility to pick one option out of many
5. generation _____	**e.** famous; having been around for a long time
6. tour guide _____	**f.** earn money for shelter, food, and other necessities
7. aunt _____	**g.** a person who shows visitors around and gives information about a place

A Cheju Diver

The island of Cheju off the coast of South Korea is known for its natural beauty. It's also known for its **volcanoes**,[1] which are no longer active. However, Cheju is also famous for something a little more unusual. It's famous for a group of legendary women divers called *haenyos*.

These women dive into the sea every day to look for seafood. It's their job, and it's difficult and very dangerous work. They make these dives without oxygen tanks. They can **hold their breath**[2] and stay underwater for up to five minutes.

---

[1] **volcano:** a mountain with a hole in the top
[2] **hold (ones) breath:** not take additional air into the body; keep air in the lungs

For hundreds of years, the women of Cheju Island have made their living from deep within the sea. They dive into the cold waters and catch octopus, abalone, and sea urchins. The seafood they catch has fed the people of Cheju for a very long time. However, the present generation of women divers on Cheju may be the last one. Things on this small island are starting to change.

Sunny Hong is part of a new generation of Cheju women. She's a tour guide. Her life doesn't depend on catching seafood from the sea. It depends on the tourists that have started visiting the island.

Sunny thinks that the job is just right for her. She says, "I wanted to find some kind of job [in] which I can use my English, and also this kind of job fit[s] my **aptitude**."[3]

---

[3]**aptitude:** *(unusual use)* natural ability or skill

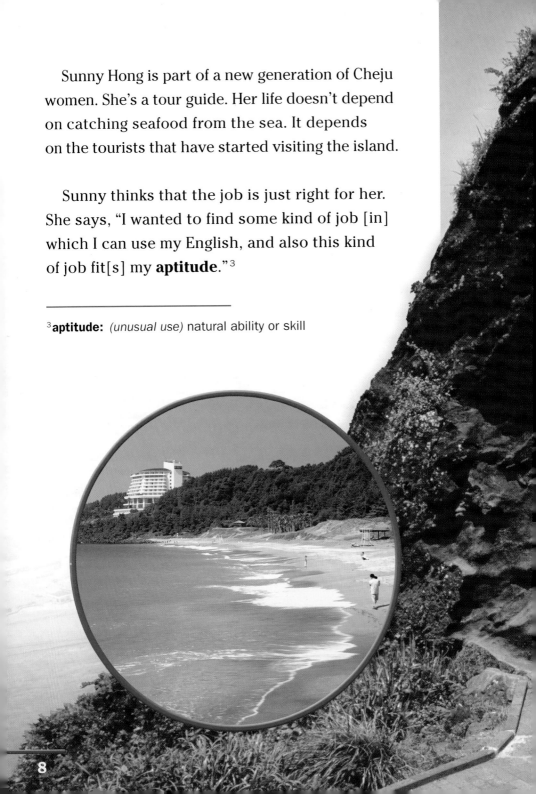

Sunny has taught herself English. It is this skill that has made her successful on land rather than having to depend on the sea. Until now, all of her female family members have worked in the sea as divers.

Sunny introduces her aunt, Ho Hong. "This is my aunt, Ms. Hong. She's 63 years old and she started diving when she was thirteen," Sunny explains, "so [she has been diving for] almost fifty years now." Sunny's aunt and her diver friends have been diving nearly all of their lives.

How did these women get started in such an unusual and sometimes dangerous job? Sunny explains for her aunt: "They didn't have a choice. Also, they were born in [a] sea village, so they had to be a woman diver, and there [was] nothing they [could] do except [be a] woman diver."

It's clear why the women didn't always choose to be divers. The job is very dangerous. In fact, it's the most dangerous job on the island, and it's only done by women. But what makes it so dangerous?

Predict

Answer the questions with 'True' or 'False'.
Then check your answers on page 15.

1. Divers often develop problems
   with their ears.

2. Divers never die underwater.

3. Divers can get serious pains in their bodies.

When they go down into the sea, the divers sometimes develop pains in their bodies. They can also experience very serious problems with their ears. Strong **tides and currents**[4] can even cause the divers to **drown**.[5] But the *haenyos* continue to dive, and they often do it for years.

This last generation of women divers is not a young one. The youngest diver on the island is 45 years old. The oldest diver is 75. These women dive for five to six hours every day. But why do they keep diving for so long?

---

[4]**tides and currents:** movements of the sea or ocean
[5]**drown:** die because of being unable to take in air while underwater

The answer is easy to understand when you look at the seafood they catch. 60-year-old Song Ho has had a good day. The seafood she has caught may make up to 300 U.S. dollars.

Diving is still a big business in Cheju and divers can make a good living doing it. It used to be the only way the women could get food for their families. However, it now also gives them a chance to educate their children for a better life. So what about the next generation? What about the younger women of Cheju?

Divers can make up to 300 U.S. dollars on a good day.

The young women of the island often think differently compared with the older generation. They know that they don't have to become divers; they can make other choices. Sunny, for example, has made the choice to be a tour guide. "I don't want to be a woman diver," she says. "I think I am **lucky**."[6]

These choices may be making life better for the younger generation of Cheju. However, the very old tradition of the *haenyo* may be **dying out**.[7] Sunny's aunt and her friends may just be the last of the Cheju women divers.

---

[6]**lucky:** fortunate
[7]**die out:** not exist any more

What do you think?

1. Do you think that Sunny is lucky?

2. Would you like to be a diver? Why or why not?

After You Read

1. Women divers _____ the island of Cheju dive into the sea every day.
   A. under
   B. from
   C. for
   D. into

2. Some people like to climb the volcanoes on the island of Cheju.
   A. True
   B. False
   C. Not in text

3. On page 7, 'they' in 'they catch' refers to:
   A. octopus, abalone and sea urchin
   B. every woman in Cheju
   C. the men of Cheju
   D. divers on the island

4. Why is Sunny Hong part of a new generation?
   A. She wants to be an English teacher.
   B. She has chosen a different life.
   C. She has an aptitude for diving.
   D. all of the above

5. Learning to speak English has helped Sunny to:
   A. find a different job.
   B. depend on the sea.
   C. be like her aunt.
   D. dive for many years.

6. On page 11, what does 'depend on' mean?
   A. want
   B. have
   C. need
   D. take

7. Choose the best heading for page 12:
   A. Women Choose to Be Divers
   B. Diving Safest Job on Island
   C. Men Choose Dangerous Job
   D. Diving is Only Option

8. Diving can be dangerous for people's ears.
   A. True
   B. False

9. On page 15, 'it' in paragraph one refers to:
   A. developing pains
   B. diving
   C. experiencing problems
   D. drowning

10. What does Song Ho probably think about diving?
   A. Diving is an easy way to make a living.
   B. You can make a lot of money diving.
   C. Tour guides make more money.
   D. all of the above

11. How did women divers better educate their children?
   A. They taught them a lot about diving.
   B. They showed them how to sell seafood.
   C. They taught them how wonderful diving is.
   D. They gave them money to study.

12. Sunny thinks she is lucky _____ she can make other choices.
   A. why
   B. for
   C. because
   D. where

A Diving Holiday!

Are you looking for a different kind of holiday?

Every year thousands of tourists visit Hawaii. Many of them stay in hotels on the Big Island. Others make a different choice. Here at Hawaii Holidays, we offer activity holidays in Hawaii that are away from the majority of the tourists. We offer scuba diving holidays around this beautiful island. Our customers spend their holidays wearing oxygen tanks and diving deep into the sea. They do this in order to look at beautiful fish and unusual plants. There are many diving sites in the Hawaiian Islands. One of the most special is Lanai Lookout on the island of O'ahu.

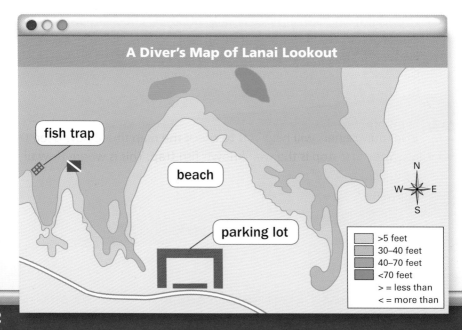

A Diver's Map of Lanai Lookout

- fish trap
- beach
- parking lot

N
W   E
S

>5 feet
30–40 feet
40–70 feet
<70 feet
> = less than
< = more than

A view from Lanai Lookout

Why should you visit O'ahu with Hawaii Holidays?

O'ahu is 150 miles north of the Big Island of Hawaii. It is home to Hawaii's biggest city, Honolulu. Our customers usually stay in Honolulu. We take them to visit the most attractive places where they can enjoy nature. Lanai Lookout is a favourite place for divers who want to experience the beauty of this island. We offer a special scuba diving visit to Lanai Lookout.

A Day at Lanai Lookout

Beginner divers are not allowed to dive here. We only take experienced divers because the sea has very strong tides and currents. It can be dangerous for a beginner. Our visit to Lanai is an unforgettable experience. You begin by walking from the car park down to the sea. Before starting your dive, our trainers will help you to check the map to see how deep the water is. Your first stop is the well-known fish trap. This is where Hawaii University catches fish for scientific studies. During the dive, our trainers will help you to stay safe. They will ensure that you stay in areas where the water is less than 40 feet deep. We promise you will love the beauty of Lanai Lookout and enjoy this special dive.

Word Count: 327
Time: _____

Vocabulary List

aptitude (8)
aunt (3, 11, 12, 19)
choice (3, 12, 19)
die out (19)
diver (2, 3, 4, 7, 11, 12, 15, 17, 19)
drown (15)
generation (3, 7, 8, 15, 16, 19)
hold their breath (4)
legendary (3, 4)
lucky (19)
make a living (3, 7, 16)
oxygen tank (2, 4)
sea (2, 8, 11, 15)
seafood (2, 4, 7, 8, 16)
tides and currents (15)
tour guide (3, 8, 19)
tourist (3, 8)
volcano (4)